RIVER FRIEND

A series of Riverine Small Books

by Sylvia M. Haslam and Tina Bone

BOOK 2

STREAM STORY I:

A Riveting Riverscape—River Brue, Somerset

Book 2

STREAM STORY I: A Riveting
Riverscape—River Brue, Somerset

A Book in a series of Riverine
publications by

Sylvia M. Haslam and Tina Bone

*Written and Edited by Sylvia Haslam and
Tina Bone. Illustrated by Tina Bone
(unless otherwise stated)*

RFS2: PAPERBACK 52pp.
ISBN No. 978 1 9162096 0 2
54 Illustrations

Published by: Tina Bone UK
First edition: September 2019
Revision 1: December 2019
Revision 2: March 2020
Revision 3: June 2020
www.riverfriend.tinasfineart.uk

CONTENTS

INTRODUCTION TO THE SERIES

Rivers are vital. They bring freshwater to the land, on which all its life depends. They are beautiful and fascinating, making up both the typical British countryside and many of its most spectacular views. If they vanished, what hardship and outrage there would be! Yet, slowly, slowly, they are vanishing, the larger stream becomes smaller, the tiny brook becomes a ditch and dries, and is filled in— the small ditches get polluted and dug out, become dull, and vanish from sight and consciousness. How can we save our rivers and riverscapes? How can we raise awareness on this slow, almost invisible loss?

We believe that this series of handy, small books, suitable for readers from teenage upwards, will help to raise awareness. Individually, each book tells a story on a particular riverine and riparian environment. Collectively, the series will inform, in a simple and effective manner, the invaluable worth of freshwater and its plants.

The Authors realised that there was a huge gap in the literature. There are many publications for scientists, for pond-dippers, birders and anglers, but "easy-read" books focussing on the river itself, and the vegetation belonging to it and creating the habitat for all else: we could find none!

For explanations regarding British freshwater plants, terminology mentioned throughout the series, and Picture Guide and reference section for further reading, see the book entitled *A PROLOGUE TO THE SERIES: Plant identification and Glossary of Terms* (also available to view free on-line at http://riverfriend.tinasfineart.uk/product/a-prologue-to-the-river-friend-series-isbn-978-1-9162096-2-6/)

Other titles in the Series are listed on the last page of this book and on the River Friend Website:
http://www.riverfriend.tinasfineart.uk

STREAM STORY I:
A Riveting Riverscape—River Brue, Somerset

Introduction

Fig. 1. Glastonbury Tor

This book is about the Somerset River Brue, which rises beyond the Somerset Levels from the Mendip Hills to the Wiltshire Downs and southwards, and, along with its tributaries, flows west to the Bristol channel. It describes a whole unit, the River Brue, intermittently from its source to its mouth: a "proper" river, composed of various brooks (Fig. 2), and has so much that is unique. Each brook comprising the Brue, the north and south Brew, the Pitt, and most of the Alham, are all fairly ordinary streams, but each has its own history. Downstream, the brooks flow together and the rivers get bigger. The Brue becomes wider and deeper, the volume of water and the upstream length and catchment are greater, so the plants inhabiting it change to those more suitable for the new depth, flow, and substrate. Generally the pollution increases as the river receives more dirty run-off from fields, roads, houses, gardens—and maybe industry.

Avalon, Glastonbury—names of myth and magic. Wells Cathedral, Glastonbury Tor (Fig. 1)—names of magnificence. Bruton, name of education, and Puriton of armaments. The Abbot's Fish House, the Cold Harbour—names of curiosity. The Abbot of Glastonbury coming home up the river from Bristol, via the River Axe from the Channel; murder and mayhem in the peatlands. All these are on the Somerset River Brue. Truly a riveting riverscape.

The myths only surfaced around the first millennium, written by William of Malmesbury (1180). Much that is great and good can in fact be inspired and created on rather dodgy foundations. Glastonbury is the only part of England with strong tales of Jesus' visit. The Glastonbury thorn is a rare variant of hawthorn which flowers in mid winter, and legend says the one at Glastonbury was the walking stick of Joseph of Arimathea, which he planted in the ground on his visit there.

Glastonbury, in the modern sense, is a popular music festival held in a muddy field near the town. For the archaeologist, amongst the most ancient English sites is the Lake Village, on stilts in what was the lake; and the Sweet Track, a causeway across the wetland.

This is also the main place of William Blake's much-loved hymn *Jerusalem* (1804).

And did those feet [Jesus Christ's] **in Ancient times** [*c.* 20 AD] **Walk upon England's mountains** [The word "mountain" has changed its meaning, and is used for much lower hills now. Today's mountains are usually brown above, changing to green in lower slopes and foothills. Mountains are not meadow-type] **green?**

And was the holy Lamb of God

On England's pleasant pastures seen? [Somerset had and has remarkable green and valuable meadows and pastures.]

And did the countenance divine

Shine forth upon our clouded hills? [clouded. This is usually read in conjunction with the dark mills of the next lines. However, it is more likely to refer to the low mist that used to cover the undrained land much of the time, and was vividly described in Victorian novels, and as seen in Figure 1. In The Fenland, Ely Cathedral was traditionally known as "The Ship of the Fens" because the low mist made the cathedral appear to be floating on it. Drained arable land has lost most of its mist.]

And was [The New] **Jerusalem builded here**

Among those dark satanic mills? [This is a change of place. The water mills round here were indeed numerous. Cheddar Gorge, for instance, had a dozen in a quarter of a mile. But with the rivers small, necessarily the mills also were small. The large (then-new, steam-powered) mills with notoriously bad working conditions were mostly in the north on such rivers as the Hodder and Calder.]

[Then the hymn ends]

…In England's green and pleasant land. [Rabbi Lionel Blue, whose family came in the 1930s as refugees from Germany, was one of the many who feel the truth of the hymn. He altered the last line to read: "In England's green and promised land" in reference to the Promised Land of the Jews in the Old Testament.]

History and Topography

What is the appropriate name for this area? The "Brue Valley Riverscape" covers it. The area may also be called the Northern part of the Somerset Wetlands, or the Somerset Levels and Moors. "Wetlands" is a definitive American term. It came to notice with the 1960s international (or European) programmes such as the International Biological Programme (Wetlands) and the Ramsar Convention. These two used different definitions of "Wetlands" and neither were the standard US definition: "those areas that are inundated or saturated by surface or ground water at a frequency and duration sufficient to support, and that under normal circumstances do support, a prevalence of vegetations typically adapted for life in saturated soils…generally include swamps, marshes, bogs, and similar areas." (United States Environmental Protection Agency). The singular "Wetland" appeared. Damp land, saturated land, shallow-flooded land, intermittently flooded land, and with ponds and lakes, and marshes—all often with drier areas of raised land. In Britain, wetlands does not normally mean the peat bog, the acid peat upland moors, which grade from drier heaths to wet Blanket bogs. Sometimes, though, these *are* included. In Somerset, "wetlands" is a most useful term, covering all the low-lying wetter areas: the Levels are on alluvium, and the Moors are on peat; "Wetlands" covers both, but excludes the upland moors of Exmoor and Dartmoor (which were once called "mosses"). There were many regional differences in the descriptive words! For example, Fen, on alkaline peat formed underwater, was mostly eastern, and inland. The Somerset lowland peats, however, are mostly near-bog ones, their peat grown above and not below water level. But because of the influx of water from the hill-rising River Brue, which is nutrient-rich and includes some pure limestone, most of the peat is not as acid and nutrient-low as that of the upland moors and bogs. (Peat is an accumulation of partially decayed vegetation or organic matter.)

Fig. 2 River Brue. The old navigable connection of the Brue is shown with a dashed line. The estates of Glastonbury Abbey are outlined in grey (Re-drawn from Rippon 2006)

The valley of the River Brue is part of the largest westward-facing wetland in Britain (Fig. 2). It drains "The South West" corner into the Bristol Channel. Its upper tributaries rise in hard or soft clay, or hard limestone, giving a pleasing variety of low hills, the ridges running out to the west, the northernmost being the High Mendips.

The present Somerset wetlands are wedge-shaped, now-damp, formerly really wet land south of Bristol reaching south to Bridgwater and north to Wales (e.g., the Gwent Levels). Since the end of the Ice Age some 8,000 years ago, there have been periods when the sea came in (marine transgressions, depositing silt, now clay) and times when the land was drier, with fresh water. This is when peat was formed.

4

The Severn Valley was drowned by the sea about 8200–5750 BC. In 5000 BC there was much salt marsh. By about 4500 BC brackish reedbed was common (marine incursion), the lowest peat being over clay, freshwater wetland, marsh or wet woodland and creating peat. This led to raised bog which lasted 5000 years until the coming of drainage and Enclosure. The peat moors were inland towards Glastonbury with much sedge and reed, fen woodland and open water. The drier woodland was mostly oak (Figs 3, 4)!

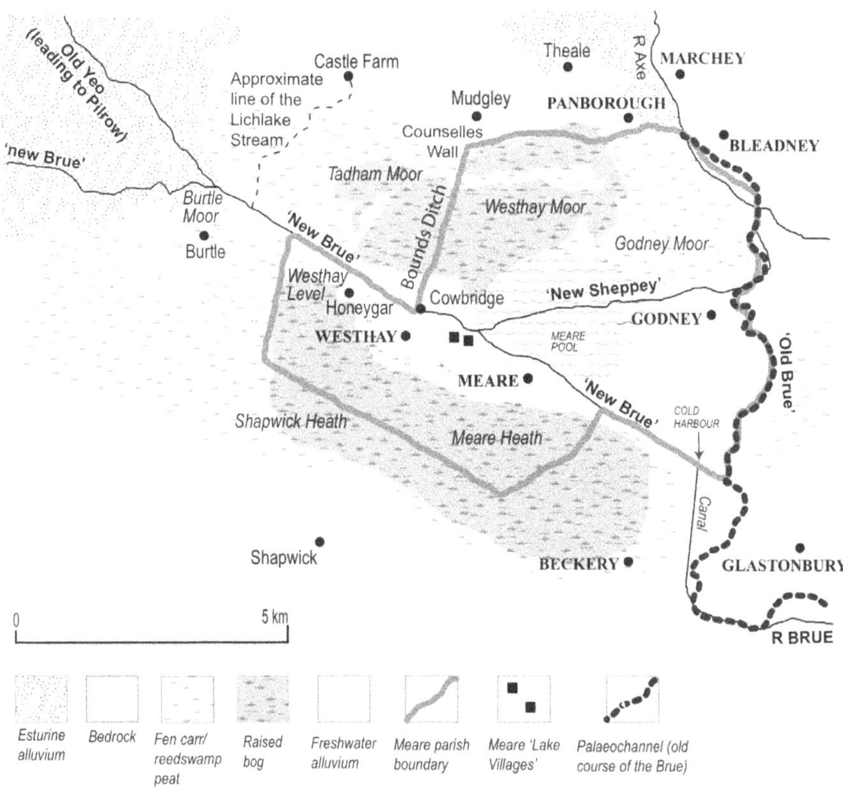

Fig. 3. Meare parish/manor and major soil-formations in the Brue and Axe Valleys. The "islands" of Glastonbury Abbey (some are actually promontories) are labelled in capitals. Note that the contemporary landscape context of the Iron-Age Meare "Lake Villages" was raised bog, which is now sealed by later alluvium deposited after the diversion of the Brue and around the fringes of the medieval Meare Pool (Re-drawn from Brunning & Farr Cox, 2005)

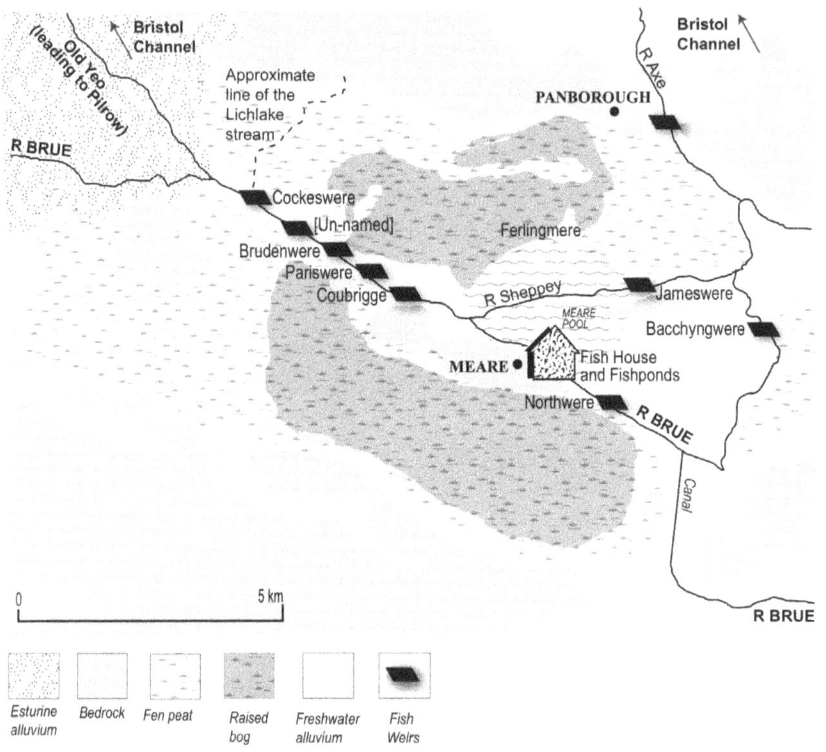

Fig. 4. Meare Pool and the locatable documented fish weirs and soils (Re-drawn from Rippon 2006)

At the end of the last Ice Age the ice sheet (glacier) had reached down to the Bristol region, but not as far as the Brue valley, although life just beyond a large ice sheet would hardly have been a hospitable environment!

There are three rivers crossing this area from east to west: the Axe to the north under the Mendip Hills, the Brue in the centre, and the southern Cary flowing to the Parrett (via the present-day King's Sedgemoor Drain, Fig. 2).

When the River Brue is first apparent, historically called the River Siger (Fig. 5) it rises in and by the wetlands with no connection to the surrounding uplands. The Siger was extant from pre-Roman into Roman and Saxon times. In the twelfth century the Welsh, who were navigating the Bristol channel near the River Axe, were calling the area "Siger". In medieval times the Siger had vanished. The Brue ran northwards to the eastern end of the flood plain, to flow into the Axe. Then, behold, another change: the Brue flowed north by Mark to the west, but still joining the Axe, then another alteration (*c.* 1300) it ran down its present course to Highbridge. Finally, more drainage was needed, and the parallel North Drain (*c.* 1800), followed by the South Drain on the Brue's other side were constructed. The Pitlow Cut made the Brue navigable to Mark, and hence to the Axe, replacing the Panborough Gap channel. By 1326 the **Hartlake River** was straightened to make the conjoined **Redlake** and **Whitelake** rivers. During the Second World War (1940) the new armaments factory at Puriton needed much water and the Huntspill River (parallel) was created, replacing the South Drain to the west. Few rivers have had such a chequered past! With such a large flood plain and changes in the relative land-level over time, rivers fluctuate, channels fluctuate, habitat fluctuates, and man-made changes fluctuate.

In about 12000 BC deciduous (mainly oak) forest was plentiful. As the ice vanished, sea level rose, and eventually salt water flowed in and the land drowned. Water level fluctuations have continued since. Ex-peat bogs, pools, reedbeds, copses and woods, and alluvial marshes all developed over time as water level rose and fell.

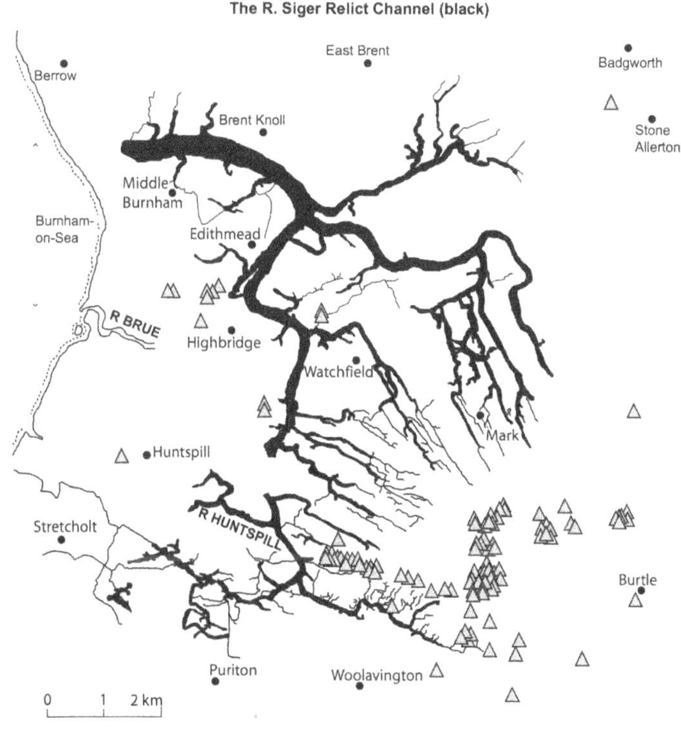

Fig. 5. Roman salterns (triangles) and some present day settlements
(Re-drawn from Brunning, R. & Far Cox, F., 2005)

People had colonised the wetlands by 5000 BC, which is when the oldest (found!) tracks across the wetlands were constructed. The earliest excavated "Lake Village" dates from 250 BC.

So what was it like by the River Siger in Roman times? There was much industry: see all the salt pans in Figure 5. It is easy for us in our high-technology times to forget, but salt is necessary for human life. Roman Britain was famous for its Cornish tin, silver, and other products as well as the mundane production of salt. Salt was deposited in a flood plain when sea level was high and salt water flooded what later became drained land.

Fig. 6. Meare: present course of the River Brue with ex-Meare Pool to the north; main road along ridge (drier) with village on each side. Drained in "oblongs". Narrow strips lead from old housing to ex-Meare Pool. Hedges along drier fields (Drawn from Aerial photograph)

Where mineral silt, etc., is deposited, alluvial clays result. Where water is clear and shallow (if other habitat factors are suitable), peat can grow. When the land dries, peat shrinks more, and can be harvested for fuel, so the peaty Moors are now mostly lower than the alluvial Levels. Figures 3, and 4 above, and Figure 6 show the present Levels and Moors distribution. This wetland is unique, though it does share some features with the other large British wetlands of the Fenland, Broads, and Trent Flood Plain, for example.

Wetlands

Flowing waters in Britain are mostly named "river", "stream" or "brook", as elsewhere (but, note well, a dictionary "stream" is any flowing watercourse: the River Severn as well as the River Pitt!).

The solitude and remoteness of much of Britain had slowly receded, particularly with the coming of the railways (1840s onwards). Who now in Torbay, if asked the time, replies in Torquay time (which, as late as the early twentieth century, was measured and set by a relative of mine) rather than Greenwich Mean Time, or British Summer Time? Similarly, with regional descriptive names, the Levels, a name unique to wetlands facing the Bristol Channel, is easily remembered: but is usually more used in the loose sense of flood plain. Similarly the peat wetlands, the Moors: but there are different upland moors of Exmoor and Dartmoor, where "moor" is embodied in the name. What is called a "sluice" in most of England is here—if old-established and (now) a landmark—a clyse or clyst. The 1940s Gold Corner one is too new. It is a "Sluice"! Drainage and irrigation channels here, man-made or man-retained, are usually rhynes, pronounced, and often spelt, "reens". However, the three most recent man-made channels are the North and South Drains (drain being an eastern term) and the Huntspill River.

"Ditch" (small) and "Drain" (large) are widespread terms. "Dyke" (Saxon, eastern) is spreading. Dyke, dijk, was originally a large man-made ditch, dug on a frontier, with a trench facing the enemy, through which raiders had to pass to reach the defenders on the ridge above, who could throw things and were in a better position to fight, for example, Offa's Dyke, Devil's Dyke. The term applied to both the low and the high part—as in, for example, Victorian Fenland, when you both walked (ridge) and boated (watercourse) along the dyke. Scottish dykes, or dikes, go up (including walls), US dikes go up, Dutch dijks are up, or both up and down. English ones are now usually just down, and with water; intermediate in size between ditch and drain.

A term, now infrequent but scattered over the country, is "cold harbour" (Fig. 7). This was a place on a navigable channel where boats could pull up. Watermen were often considered the dregs of society (until the railways much diminished their number), and having them in respectable neighbourhoods could be considered shocking. In Cambridge, England, for instance, a causeway was built along the centre of the River Cam between the University Colleges so that the ears of the undergraduates might not be sullied by the ungentlemanly language of the watermen. So cold harbours developed: not the warm, hospitable inns scattered along the watercourses for the more respectable (and rich), but places where water men could camp. The Glastonbury Cold Harbour was far enough away that rowdy behaviour would not bother the Abbot (one of the Great Men of the land, pre-Reformation). In Taunton, a mere merchant town, it was close to the centre.

Fig. 7. Cold Harbour (now just open land) near Glastonbury, River Brue

What were the wetland living conditions like? That depended on the period in time, the state of the sea level, and the political fortunes of the day. In general, the dry, landed side of the Brue catchment followed the fortunes and health of the rest of the county. The wetlands, in Neolithic times, were at least in part excellent, despite the swampy nature of the Lake Village (on stilts) which must have encouraged "ague" (malaria or another illness involving fever and shivering), rheumatism, and water-borne diseases. In Roman times, the large number of saltpans showed not only previous seawater incursions, but the efficiency of the Roman engineers in extracting salt. Glastonbury Abbey was founded by about 600 AD, and its site on the high Tor (tors are

10

small rocky mounts in this region) in the middle of wetland, was obviously well-placed for defence. The Abbey also owned much of the most productive grasslands with water (flood lands) and, because of its isolation, received low interference from King or Council. But the Abbot of Glastonbury did not have it all his own way. The Bishop of Wells too had his See near, and even the Prior of Wells came in on the act with independent lands.

A little "kingdom" could and did develop. So, particularly after *c.* 1000 AD, did myth and legend, greatly encouraging pilgrims and therefore wealth.

Wealth came to those living around in both the wetland and the lowland, and higher on the Mendip Hills.

Figure 6 shows how the flood plain was drained early in oblongs (records include twelfth century!). This adds greatly to wealth, but takes time. Originally such channels were a winding network, changing with the flood and sea movements. Of course they changed with the attempts to drain, to flood, to cut peat, fell trees, and harvest fish or crops. It usually took centuries to develop these neat oblongs. But the medieval times were the climatic optimum of the Sub-Atlantic.

Both investment and husbandry lessened in the late Middle Ages. The Dissolution of the monastery of Glastonbury was in 1535. The Abbey had centuries of experience in managing both wet and dry land, and doing so as a unit. Now it was split up, and became less productive.

Drainage progressed (and declined) responding to habitat, investment and expertise (Fig. 8). Tensions between landowner drainers (for crops) and wetlanders (for fish, fowl, peat, etc.) varied between amicable and murderous. By and large it was the local peasants who were wetlanders, taking advantage of all the crops the Levels could offer, living a near self-sufficient life, without much liking or wish for interference from outsiders. Generally it was the outsiders who had the capital to drain and replace the multifarious wetland crops with the plush grass of grazing land as shown, for example, in Figure 10a below.

By the time Victorian social conscience arrived, semi-industrial farmland could be imposed. The Victorian moralists saw that these new agricultural practices enabled peasants to become paid agricultural labourers. Houses belonging to landlords could be built and repaired, tumbledown shacks could go. Their inhabitants were to be labourers, not peasants, not just visiting their own fish-lines (most fishing, though, was on an individual basis), peat diggings or vegetable patches, but working full-time on others' property. This opened the way for children to attend school, thus improving health, and resulting in increased wealth which provided adequate clothing, etc.. The Levels folk slowly became part of rich and "civilized" Somerset.

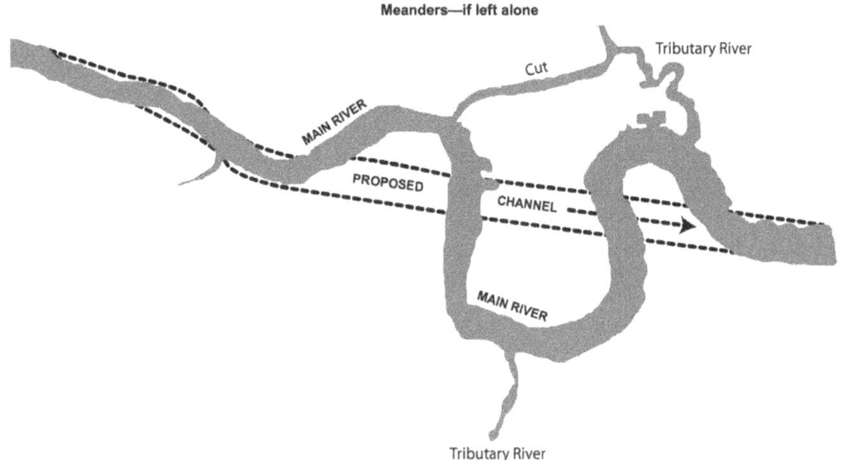

Fig 8. Proposed channel (typical) to shorten river, quicken flow, and release more land for cultivation

However good these material things were, the social change included the loss of an independent and self-sufficient way of life that was enviable. Over to the east in the Fenland, the fen ague, considered to be a form of malaria, was rife, and even into the twentieth century Cambridge chemists sold opium "for the ague" (and other ills). This obviously added greatly to the malaise, desire for idleness, and squalor of these independent folk. (Identification of the malarial mosquito parasite was only discovered after the disease had been effectively eradicated, by drainage and better hygiene practices.)

Hemp, a variety of cannabis, grows well in fens and was used both to make ropes, which was well-approved by authority and as a recreational drug, which was not. Given the difficulty of keeping clean and sanitary in wet conditions, cannabis encouraged squalor and lethargy. Oddly, although fen ague in The Fenland was generally important to eighteenth and nineteenth century writers, it was not so in the Somerset Levels. Were the diseases just the water-borne ones or were they dirt-encouraged typhoid, typhus, rheumatism, smallpox, arthritis, etc.? Even cholera (waterborne, nineteenth century, and with horrifying epidemics) is not important in the literature related to the Somerset area.

12

The raised land around and within the Levels (Fig. 9) was the place to build. This avoided flooded houses (in old houses, their base reflects the flood level of the district at the time when they were built), and was healthier.

Fig. 9. River Brue looking to Glastonbury. Rhyne. Water level below ground

The Riverscape of the River Brue

There is far too much of the River Brue of great interest to describe it all here in such a small book, so only a few areas have been selected and described. The name "Bruton" is the town (ton) on the River Brue. Brewham (North and South), is the hamlet (small village) upstream. There is Brue Farm (well downstream of Bruton) and other places connected with the river name. Upstream to the north is a landscape basin, where northern tributaries rise. There is also an oval vale running roughly from north (near Frome) to south (Fig. 10a). There are several small streams combining to form the River Frome in the north and the River Brue in the south. These receive run-off from the vale slope above. Land, as well as wetland and pools, was drained by two main methods: above and below ground. Above-ground drainage was by shortened, deepened and straightened brooks so that water could flow to the main channels quicker. Also, by deepening the channels, ground water is usually lowered, and drainage aided. This has been done in some areas and often inefficiently over centuries, but has been regulated and expanded greatly over the past two centuries (Fig. 10b).

Fig. 10a. Looking to the oval vale from which the River Brue rises and flows to the south (right) and the River Frome to the North

Fig. 10b. Highbridge, River Brue. Upstream clyst. Freshwater

South Brewham still has perennial stream flow, and there is an ex-watermill: "One mill mentioned in the *Domesday Book* was probably located close to the bridge which crossed the River Brue, on the site where later mills were built." (A Short History of Brewham). The stream is 2–3m wide and usually shallow in summer. Water level was historically higher than it is now, naturally, and higher again because of the construction of weirs for mills, fish, etc.. There was ample water depth for small boats, pulled up or poled by a horse or man, alongside or within the stream. Row-boat-sized barges were commonly used for freight on slowish streams over 2m wide. This was often easier, so cheaper, than the alternative of carriers on bad roads (the ruts and water on roads were horrendous—see *The Pilgrim's Progress* by John Bunyan—and you could drown in road pools!); though the carriers also, where width and water depth permitted, could travel along stream beds (Figs 11, 12).

Fig. 11. South Brewham, downstream River Brue, Old mill, etc..

Fig. 12. Brewham, upstream of Fig. 11, former wharf, now garden.

There is evidence of Stone Age and Bronze Age activity here—the geology determining its location. A broad band of Oxford Clay runs north to south and underlies the eastern part of the parish, with a wooded escarpment on Kimmeridge Clay forming its eastern boundary and, at the top, Greensand (sandstone). From South Brewham to the western boundary, running north to south, are two types of limestone: first a narrow band of Cornbrash, on which Brewham was first settled, followed by a band of Forest Marble.

Domesday Book tells us that in 1066 Brewham was held by Robert, son of Wimarc, but that Norman King William granted it to William de Mohun. In 1086, 'Briweham' is recorded to have 2 mills, 17 cattle, 60 pigs, 300 sheep, three riding horses and 22 wild mares. The population was just under one hundred. Before he died in 1176, de Mohun's grandson gave all his land north of the Brue, together with his estate at Horseley south of the river, to the canons of Bruton, including Combe Brook with its many potential mill sites. After the dissolution of the monasteries in 1539 the estate passed to the Crown and was subsequently sold to the Berkeleys of Bruton.

The change from Oxford clay to limestone marked the edge of the Royal Forest of Selwood. The bridge across the Brue in South Brewham, recorded in 1219, was the first public crossing of the river where it emerged from the forest, and it is likely that the present bridge may have moved from its original position. One of the mills mentioned in *Domesday Book* was probably located close to the original bridge, on the site where later mills were built.

Bruton is a fascinating town. The River Brue here—now a small river 4–8m wide—allowed a merchant town to develop. There is the standard pattern of a bridge (most old bridges are traditionally arched to allow for the easy passage of boats and floodwaters), an ex-ford, ex-wharf, ex-market place which is the original and typical basis for the development of an English settlement. This would have been the original site. (See Figs 13–17.) Expansion led to further streets and a second bridge. Ultimately this led to more industry in the literal sense, i.e. not handmade, so to increased wealth, for traders and merchants and the providers for all other goods found rurally. Wealth was not excessive, but enough to allow a "comfortable" living. The High Street is also typical, with the houses running near-parallel, and above, the river (too high for normal floods). Stepping stones give another way to cross the river—it is now rare to find them (Fig. 18).

The river, now 8–12m wide, was fully wide enough for freight and transport boats in plenty. The early nineteenth century canalisation came up to Bruton from Highbridge (so leading to Bristol and other British and foreign ports).

Fig. 13. Bruton, looking south from main bridge

Fig. 14. Bruton, River Brue, downstream

Fig. 15. Bruton, upstream site of main bridge, River Brue. Old wharf, pump (far), old inn and perhaps harbour control

Fig. 16. Bruton, River Brue

16

Fig. 17. Bruton, River Brue, clay stream

Fig. 18. Bruton, River Brue, upstream. Old (but re-done) stepping-stone crossing

Naturally, purpose-made canals are more efficient commercially than this sort of river, but Bruton survived.

Look for mills! There were several mills (at least 5) big and small. Mills increased spinning and weaving capacity. North of the river were the mills which were dependent on the limestone hills. There were six mills by Domesday (1086).

King Canute sited a Royal Mint at Bruton.

On the map, Bruton is clearly the "capital" of a sub-section of Somerset. Why here rather than any other expanding village? Because of a combination of ample water—the Brue does not dry in summer, with reasonable access by boat. If access had been good, Bruton might have been a county or vice-county town. Whilst ample water and reasonable access by boat applies also to various other villages in the region, in addition, Bruton had a plentiful supply of limestone water to turn mill wheels and develop products (e.g., from the Combe Brook).

North of Bruton are limestone Downs. Combe Brook and its tributaries were fully used, so factories could be developed—and they prospered. (The first mills [pre-Domesday] were mainly flour ones. Much diversification came in early medieval times, with a further great expansion in the eighteenth century. The nineteenth century brought widespread steam power, so water power, though still much used, was no longer necessary.)

Looking around Bruton, there is an odd feature. The number of schools seems excessive. This is a good example of how important for centuries one man can be. Mr Hugh Sexey, auditor to both Henry VIII and Elizabeth I had, as was typical in Tudor times, not only served his country well, but made his own fortune, which he left to his home town, for good schooling (amongst other good works like building an almshouse). Bruton is still a centre for good schools, a fact which cannot be deduced from its geography!

The classic early pattern of a river-based village/town has been overlaid in this instance by the combined influence of the Combe Brook and Mr Sexey, but a river town has developed with Church, ford (then bridge), wharf, civic building, then High Street (comfortably-off residents), mills (River Brue and tributaries) and residential and industrial infill.

Moving downstream through pleasant English lowlands, various tributaries flow into the River Brue passing various old river villages. Lydford-on-Fosse illustrates the early importance of trade and wealth (Fig. 19), and Bruton's rapid development prevented later development here. Here also is the old bridge (crossing place), the church, and a large wharf/market place. However, such further development as occurred was more influenced by the nearby Fosse Way, a major prehistoric, (and later) Roman highway.

Fig. 19. Lydford. River Brue. Large market place/Wharf near side of Church

Where river and road meet, goods (and people) could be transferred from one to the other. Therefore this was an important junction: so a large market place for storing goods until collection!

Baltonsborough has an old watercourse bypass. This long village was clearly built along the Brue and would have been a medium-sized port. However, it did not flourish enough to spare it from the straightened, well-dug, shorter channel constructed as a bypass. From here downstream (Fig. 20) the river is clearly man-made, straight, soon flowing into the moors (peatlands) of the upper wetland (by Butt, Kennard and South Moors). The moors are heavily drained, and are now mostly rich farmland.

Fig. 20 Near Baltonsborough, River Brue, clay vegetation, cut off (canalised) bypass

Glastonbury had its own tributary, the Tor being large enough to support springs, including those containing red iron or white lime. The river cut through low ground beside the Tor, but its present course is obviously man-managed, if not man-made. The then tiny town incorporating the monastery and its supporting traders and workers had plenty of spring water. The Brue was used for navigation and alongside the town the channel was previously commercial, but with new commercial now there too. Where the river turns away from the town is the site of the Cold Harbour where the watermen could "park" and stay well away from the sober, discreet (or at least officially so!) precincts of the Abbey.

The Abbey, dating back to at least 600 AD, owned much land, dry, drained and wet. The Abbot was a power in the land, so much property provided much work on and around the land, and consequently involved much administration. After the Abbey's Dissolution in about 1535 this unified and intensive management was lost. The Abbey had, of course, responsibilities and contacts outside Somerset, both nationally and internationally. Horsemen and pedestrians had difficulty, until maybe the eighteenth century when new turnpike roads (on which tolls were charged) were introduced. Roads were often poor and even "abominable" according to John Bunyan's *Pilgrims Progress*, 1694. Travel by water was available and was usually quicker, safer and more comfortable. Journeys from the Abbey first went to near what is now Weston-super-Mare, the mouth of the River Axe. Most traffic would then go along the coast to what is now Avonmouth, then up the River Avon to Bristol (watching for tides!). From there boats could go up the River Avon, and if including short land journeys, link to the Thames, London, and thence all of Britain and the European continent. Or there was a moderately* good road to London. *(* "Moderately": it is recorded that some merchants in medieval times had a special service in Bristol Cathedral to pray for a safe journey to London!)*

But how did boats get from the River Brue at Glastonbury to Weston-super-Mare? For most of the Abbey's history the main route was not directly down to Highbridge (see the River Siger, Fig. 5) but over to the River Axe (see Fig. 2); and this not just by one route, but by two. First by a no-longer-navigable (indeed nearly lost) channel east of Wedmore through Horton (Panborough Gap, Fig. 2) and later the still marked and extant channel by Mark. A causeway is a constructed, raised Way over wetland or water, and Mark Causeway crosses this with its canal.

Mark is interesting. The man-made canal has an unmistakable, though small, waterfront (Fig. 21). The canal goes round the west of the Wedmore Ridge, up through Rooks Bridge, and on into the River Axe. North of Mark the influence of management is obvious. Two parallel channels cross the moor. Where is the once-sharp difference between the navigable canalised river and the drain? Without boats, the channels were managed alike and became alike (Fig. 22).

Fig. 21. Mark. Corner, old River Brue branch going north to River Axe. Replacement water front

Fig. 22. Mark, old River Brue branch, later canalised to River Axe Levels. Village and church on higher ground

The later channel west of Glastonbury is man-made, navigation-friendly, passing through the peat Moors and, downstream, the alluvial (and higher) Levels near Highbridge. Meare pool ("Meare", a variant of "mere", is a large pool or lake), was drained in the eighteenth century—that century of "improvements". The village is ancient, but grew along the river. It has the unique Abbot's Fish House (Figs 23–24) an odd, chapel-like building, two storeys high, but with no indoor access to the upstairs, just a wooden stairway outside. It just sits on raised ground near, but not on, either a pool or a river.

Fig. 23. The Fish House at Meare as pictured by J.C. Buckler in 1828, showing the first floor stairs and garderobe extension (on the left), all no longer extant. Meare Pool (fish pond) beyond (Re-drawn from Brunning, 2006)

Fig. 24. The Abbots Fish House, Meare, in 2017. River Brue

The building is recorded from the fourteenth century as being a fish house. Fish were pressed in the lower storey and there were small fish ponds around, presumably to keep fish alive and fresh, until required.

This was mystifying if compared with monastery fish houses in, for example, France (Dombes) and the Czech Republic, Trĕbon, (Fig. 25). Here the design has a reason. Ponds have semi-regulated water levels, so it was possible to build houses in shallow water which had ground floors flooded deep enough to store live fish (with water movement in and out of the house to keep it oxygenated). The fishkeeper lived on the first floor. This was a sensible and practical arrangement (before freezers). So why build the fish house above the river at Meare? It is possible that Glastonbury's architects, being a long way from the central continent, could have misinterpreted the instructions received about the positioning of the fish house: it should have been in the pool!

Fig. 25. Czech Republic,Trĕbon. Fish House (no longer used), note below-water entrance for bringing in fish to store (and to change taste) prior to sale, and upper entrance for keeper. Summer water level low. In winter, water level higher, and entry is by the stairs to the first floor

It is difficult to describe the intricate wetlands channels as tributaries of the River Brue. They are man-made or man-managed drains. The North and South Drains are the main channels, which have innumerable ditches and dykes (rhynes) across the wetland.

The South Drain was built as a canal (Fig. 26). It now ends at Gold Corner (Fig. 27), where it continues as the Huntspill River (Fig. 28), taking the water to the sea but originally ran itself to the sea with navigation. Huntspill River and Gold Corner sluice and pumping station were built to regulate the confluence of these and the lesser channels during the early World War Two years, and greatly aided draining and reduced winter flooding. The river was the last of the Great Diggings and was constructed so that great quantities of water could reach the armaments factory at Puriton. River Huntspill is the largest of these rivers. The North Drain was built near the start of the eighteenth century, with pumping increasingly necessary over time.

The railway running beside the South Drain was opened in 1854 and ran until the Beeching rail cuts in the 1960s.

In Highbridge there are the remains of an inadequate waterfront—neither a major fishing village nor an important river port. By the lower part of the River Brue, above the sluice, a terrace of small houses lines the road, presumably built for those working on the boats or in the port (Fig. 29). A pool-harbour lies behind. The start of the salt water, the tidal limit, is marked by a large sluice (Fig. 30), the original being old enough to be called a "clyse". Of course this waterfront is not ancient (River Siger and River Axe) nor well-developed later, but was very busy during the eighteenth century.

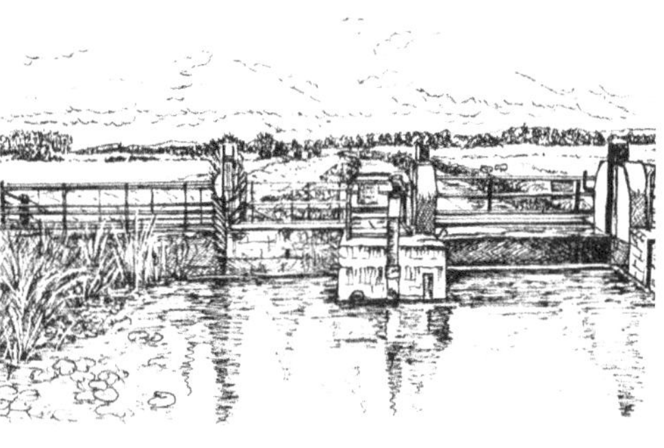

Fig. 26. Gold Corner. Upstream of controls, South Drain

Fig. 27. Gold Corner: Sluice and Pumping Station (1940)

Fig. 28. Gold Corner, downstream of controls (Huntspill River)

Fig. 29. Highbridge, waterfront. River Brue (river to right)

Fig. 30. Highbridge, River Brue. Tidal, downstream of clyst. Clyse edge shown

Underdrainage is the drainage of soil by means of gutters placed beneath the surface, recently with pipes in; formerly, often with brush. Underdrainage became widespread in the nineteenth century, and continues into the twenty-first century. Whilst "land drainage" can usually be located and understood by maps, ground study and aerial photographs, underdrainage is far more difficult to determine and identify. Not being cheap, though, it may be traceable through farm accounts. (It could be assumed that most lowland farmed land has been both drained and underdrained.) The upland brooks contain water by the time they reach the Brewhams. The upper brooks do not have perennial flow.

In undrained Exmoor and Dartmoor, the blue lines of brooks on the one-inch OS maps all have water in them, and indeed brooks or rills may continue upstream of where they are marked.

So, why are channels in intensively managed or populated areas different to those in undrained, more remote land? Land drainage means less water storage there and more and quicker run-off. With all the new, higher-yielding crop varieties, the absence of those chosen for doing well in wetter soil is con-spicuous. Allowing soil and subsoil to again become saturated soaks up a lot of water, which can later flow out slowly, so greatly decreasing flash floods. (In late Victorian times, if an invalid wanted to move house, and a local doctor was consulted, he might well suggest an area of free-draining soil, like gravel or limestone. A dry house was likely to be a healthy house.)

Conversely, out on the land, this loss of water lowered the level in the ground which water usually reached. So, the water in dips in the ground, which collected into little rills, then brooks, no longer existed (except in major storms) and the flowing upper waters therefore dried. Perennial water now flows only well below the sources.

Main Tributaries

Whilst the lower Brue flows through flat wetlands, where incoming tributaries have been channelled and straightened, the upper Brue rises in higher ground where the natural streams flow at the bottom of gentle valleys. The principal ones are marked on Figure 2.

The first stream entering the River Brue at Bruton is the Combe Brook. This rises in limestone Downs so has clear, flowing water which historically

24

powered many mills. Next downstream is the (clay) River Pitt which enters from the south of the Brue, so is more nutrient-rich. The River Pitt has much dried since its upper feeder watercourses were mapped in *c.* 1900. Further downstream, entering from the north of the River Brue is the River Alham, mostly on clay, but with some limestone upstream of the Batcombe area, and a depauperate flora—because of less water.

No other large tributaries enter the Brue until it reaches the former Meare Pool, which received two: the River Whitelake a little north of Meare, and River Sheppey, further north again. Finally there is the former navigable connection to the River Axe.

The River Whitelake is a mixed river, rather like a miniature River Brue, though without such historical interest. It rises in the higher ground to the west of Evercreech, flows west and enters flat, drained wetlands west of Pilton through which a brook runs.

Downstream, the next brook comes from the Warminster Hills (all of 130m, 500ft high!) and is a pretty little stream. It is linked to the River Sheppey— but not by a now-navigable channel. But why? It is not obvious from the map. The River Whitelake enters the flat moors, its erstwhile flood plain, downstream of Westholme (through Queens' Sedgemoor, Splotts' Moor, etc.).

The River Sheppey, the last Brue tributary flowing into the ancient Meare Pool, rises in the limestone found to Shepton Mallet ("Shep" means "sheep"). This is on the prehistoric Fosse Way, and is the site of a Roman Army settlement. (Commonly, Roman towns were on higher ground, Anglo Saxon ones down by a river crossing.) Once more, the upper brook is generally dry. By Croscombe there is much ancient industry (Fig. 31), perennial limewater flow, and (depauperate) chalkstream vegetation. Dinder, the next village downstream, has an artificial waterfront, and a river (Fig. 32a, b). This is sited well above the valley base, and may well have been a watercourse made for a mill (leat) or irrigation, easier boating, or suchlike. Proper navigation started here but such a channel is no longer continuous because it was originally interspersed with downstream Mills, etc..

The limestone Chilcote stream rises in a series of springs along the edge of the Mendip Hills and flows in to the Brue downstream of Wells (Figs 33–36) which, as its name suggests, grew up around a series of springs known as the St Andrews Risings. The water from St Andrews Spring was given by Bishop

Fig. 31. Croscombe. Ancient mill remains, etc., River Sheppey

Fig. 32a. Dinder. "Artificial waterfront" by the road leading to connecting channel, not shown

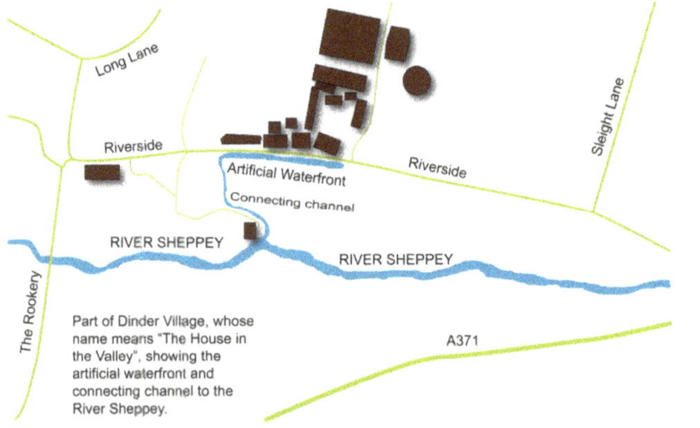

*Fig. 32b.
Schematic
diagram of
Dinder,
showing River
Sheppey
(valley),
connecting
channel, and
"waterfront"
by the road*

Beckynton (1390–1465) in the fifteenth century to supply the people of Wells with good fresh water permanently. The Bishop, and to a lesser extent, the Dean of Wells was a large landowner; less grand than the Abbot of Glastonbury, and without all his excellent meadows, but still with large lands. This also means a large workforce to work and administer the lands, and to fight with the retainers—Abbot or Prior.

These springs collectively carry water primarily from the Mendip Hills, which takes several days to reach them, via aquifers, after heavy rain. Rainwater filters through the rock below and emerges, low-nutrient and lime-rich, having been soaked in the hard carboniferous limestone. The water from the springs is collected and directed to form the moat around the Bishop's Palace. In early times the original purpose of a moat was for defence. Here the moat could be used for supply, waste disposal, mills, fish and waterfowl (the swans ring a bell to be fed!), and recreation (boating and swimming).

Fig. 33. Wells. Moat of Bishops Palace (Chilcote Stream)

Fig. 34. Wells. Ex-millstream (River Brue)

Fig. 35. Wells. Chilcote Stream to left, old ex-industry

Fig. 36. Wells, downstream of Fig. 35, new industry, by, but not belonging to stream

At the south west corner of the Bishop's Palace the Chilcote stream joins the main—though now smaller—watercourse and starts its journey to the River Sheppey. In this reach the stream was clean and used for water supply to the Bishop's Palace, Cathedral, City, and their dependents. From this point it could be dirtied as here there are remnants of old industry. There are many small industries, mills, workshops, including one chapel (there is a recent chapel too). This road is well worth walking along and studying. At the far end, the stream bends sharp right, into new commerce and industry. This forms a nice contrast. The stream is less canalised, the buildings are far larger and, whilst they are beside the river, unlike the old industry they are not reliant on the river.

Another water-related feature is the (probably) seventeenth century street drainage and cleaning (Fig. 37). This has been re-worked. Between the cathedral and the Bishop's Palace, the main road and entrance to the city has stone gutters on each side. These were fed with running water from the springs and were intended for water supply and to carry away waste and keep the street (moderately) clean. This was a state-of-the-art system, found in various other towns such as Cambridge and Salisbury.

Fig. 37. Wells. Supply/drainage road channel (from limestone stream). Re-worked

The Chilcote stream rises in the Mendips outliers to the east of its main range, but it remains small until the junction with the city springs of Wells. The main tributary has dried a lot because of land drainage. However, the city stream has kept more water because limestone is porous, allowing good drainage. Rain on the Mendips percolates through and—not being greatly abstracted or dried—still flows to the city springs.

Downstream of Wells, the Chilcote Stream and River Sheppey are not now canalised. They join in Coxley, which also had a sizeable mill. So far, outside built-up areas the streams have followed a fairly natural straight course. Shortly, however, the ground falls from lowland to flat moors, and the Sheppey starts its own, natural convoluted way down to the former Meare Pool.

There are bridges of many eras in the Brue catchment. Originally they were of the "packhorse" type, resembling that shown in Figure 38a, and were no doubt replaced on the Brue long ago. Bridges downstream of Glastonbury necessarily were constructed later than the canalised river. Large (short narrow-boat-size) boats came upstream to Bruton (see Fig. 19), and Figures 13–18 (Bruton) show the wharfs in their typical location near church and bridge). Smaller ones came up to South Brewham (as shown in Figure 12), and presumably, as elsewhere, punts or (towed) rowing boats, carrying freight came further upstream.

Fig. 38b. Another type of bridge: The Tarr Steps "Clapper" Bridge, Exmoor, Somerset

Fig. 38a. A regular type of "Packhorse" bridge (not River Brue): Gallox Bridge—A medieval packhorse bridge at Dunster, Somerset (A Packhorse bridge does still exist just a little way from the main bridge in Bruton—Fig. 13)

Products

Throughout recorded history, Somerset has been a rich county, with pockets of poverty and centuries of hardship certainly but, overall, wealth. Associated with the River Brue are several currently termed "Powerhouses", for example, the farm which holds the Glastonbury Music Festival most years.

(1) **Meadows and pastures** (Fig. 39a, b). Meadow, mown, **"One Man went to Mow, went to Mow a Meadow"**. Pasture, grazing, **"The Lord's my shepherd…(sheep) He leadeth me into green pastures"**. Much grassland was—and is—both: mown in early summer, then grazed (or variations thereof).

Fig. 39a (above), b (below). Wetland, Levels (rhynes and farm bridge)

(2) **Other land crops**, including arable, timber, orchards (cider), vineyards (medieval), flax, beans and brush.

(3) **Wetland and river produce** (see below), and rhynes, cuts, field outlines, historic peat workings, etc..

(4) **Drainage**. The high rainfall of 2012 led to damaging floods. Because of the general drying, channels had not had their previous dredging regime, and this greatly exacerbated the floods and farmers asked that dredging be re-instated. It was rumoured that the "Government" did not want to do this, and allocated £800,000 to persuade the farmers they were exaggerating, and that action was unnecessary. If that was true, it backfired because in 2016 flooding was again bad, and some dredging was re-instated. It is odd that so many people, on being told that (excluding climate change) such floods are likely to recur every century, or two centuries, automatically assume they will recur ONLY after 200 years, and do not reflect that returning next year is just as likely!

(5) **Water** is also produce—for domestic use (food, drinking, irrigation, farm, power, fish habitat, transport medium).

(6) **Religion and industry**, for example, Wells.

(7) **Manufacture and education**, for example, Bruton

(8) **Religion**, for example, Glastonbury and Wells.

Produce from the Levels ranged from fish, reeds and rushes from wetland, to arable and timber on higher and drier ground. For example: osiers (baskets, fences, furniture, general farm, boats, etc.); alders and other wetland trees, reed (building, fences, bedding, canoes); pasture, meadow; cultivated land (timber); grasses and sedges, [other] herbs; boat travel; watering cattle; piggeries; water (Water cress, etc.); vegetables (small gardens can grow and produce much fruit and vegetables near rivers); peat (turbary, the right to cut peat, hence turves and peat blocks). Turf Moors were areas of moor allocated for peat cutting.

- *Past products:* Beaver (up to medieval); Otters (up to *c.* 1950); Swans (separate from other waterfowl as they were a Royal Bird).

- *New products:* Recreational tourism, visiting the Mendips and Levels in general, nature reserves, visitor centres and historic buildings. The hospitality sector is flourishing. There may now be no watermen in the riverside pubs, but there are many cars in their car parks!

- *Local crafts* sell well in the visitor centres and local shops, whether they be books like this one, or crafts made from local osiers (and imports). Conferences and other meetings are numerous in visitor centres and village halls, bringing in revenue particularly to the Levels, Wells and Glastonbury. Ecological bird and other natural history walks and outings also bring paying visitors. Even non-paying visitors often visit cafés and gift shops.

- *Boats* were in general use for many centuries but only a few small ones remained in the 1950s. Many were made in the farms, some bought from elsewhere. Boats could be towed, pushed, sailed and be flat-bottomed or keeled. They were used for fishing, travel, freight and visiting traps. Spears, nets and dip nets were available and fish houses on the shore (see Abbots Fish House, above).

- The oldest *track* was known to have existed around 3000 BC. A track dating to 2500 BC has been excavated. The Post Track is 1840 BC, at the start of Neolithic farming and settled life—grazing, arable, wild food. As the land got wetter, later tracks became more substantial. Around 250–50 BC, lake villages were in swamps, not in water. Good craftsmen were present. Food included: perch, roach, trout, eels and other fish, otters, frogs, numerous types of duck, pelicans, cranes, beavers (to the early Middle Ages), swans, herons and bitterns; and vegetables and non-wetland birds. Interestingly, Glastonbury Abbey kept bees.

- *Salt, peat and pill boxes*. The Romans mined salt (see Fig. 5) and ores such as tin and silver. Cornwall was well known for tin earlier in Phoenician times and salt production increased in the two centuries post-Roman.

  In the second half of the twentieth century, peat abstraction vastly expanded with machine cutting. This removed not just habitat, but the history and archaeology stored in the peat. The loss was replaceable when peat was growing and the population was low. Not now!

  Peat was also used in a mix of substrates for air strips for small RAF stations which made an excellent surface on which the planes, which were light and few, could land safely during the Second World War.

  During this War also, two chains of defensive pill boxes (concrete square buildings with a look-out, a few soldiers, telescopes and a telephone to warn of invasion) were built. One chain formed an outer ring for the defence of Bristol, from the coast, up through Meare and Wells; the other ran across the peninsula from Bridgwater to the south coast.

An impressive list. So many centres of excellence along one, fairly minor, river.

Fishing

The number of fish is now greatly reduced compared with what it was pre-1800. It is very difficult now to visualise this quantity, that previously almost everywhere streams were generally unpolluted, and that the fish were usually fit to eat. The historic river fishery shown in Figure 40 is of a sixteenth century German mill and fish pond. The number of ways in which fish are being caught, and indeed the number and size of the fish, is worth noting. Figure 4 shows the number of fish weirs on just a small section of the River Brue, and Figure 41 shows the complex structure of these on the much larger River Severn. Population density in the Brue valley was low so it is likely that much fish would have been exported. The three main river landowners were churchmen in Anglo Saxon, Medieval and early Tudor times: the Abbot of Glastonbury, the Bishop, and the Dean of Wells. Church rules on avoiding meat—but allowing fish and beaver—were strict (for Advent, Lent, Fridays, sometimes Wednesdays and eves of various holy days).

Fig. 40. Re-drawn sixteenth-century German woodcut.
Mill, leat, several different means of fishing, boats

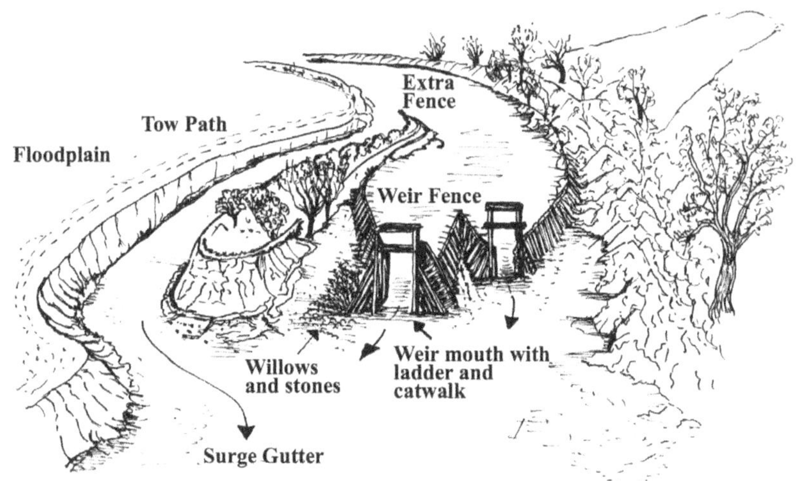

**Above: A typical fish weir on the River Severn (not to scale)
Below: Surviving and abandoned fish weir sites shown by
O.S. six-inch maps revised 1902.**

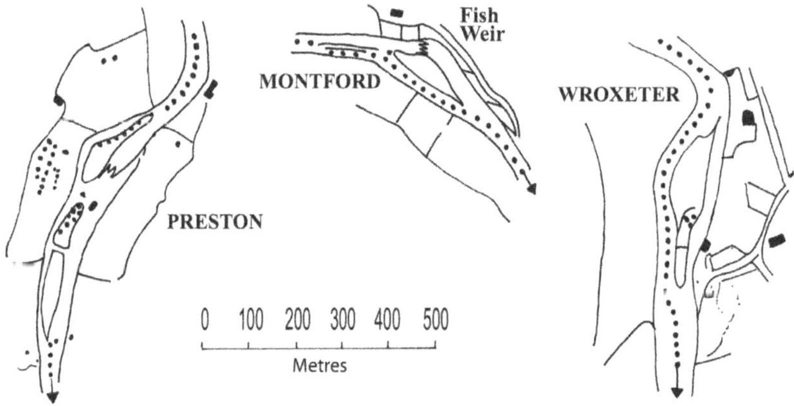

*Fig. 41. Re-drawn from Pannett, D.J. (1981). Fish weirs of the River Severn.
In Evolution of marshland landscapes. University Department of External Studies, Oxford, 144–157*

Fish loss came from several causes:

(1) **Water loss.** Rivers are shallower than they were. Irrespective of quantity, when water is held up at frequent intervals, necessarily it is deeper (it may even be toe-to-tail, and held up from one weir or sluice to the next). When navigation takes precedence over prevention of flooding, water is deeper (boats must pass, flood is irrelevant).

(2) **Water quantity**, channel size and shape also affect depth.

(3) Another type of water loss is **loss of whole streams**. Often, in lowlands particularly, the upper couple of miles or so of what used to be, according to the Ordnance Survey, flowing water, so water habitat is lost, together with all its (even small) fish and aquatic vegetation.

(4) **Abstraction**, from surface water (river, lake) or underground water (aquifer).

(5) **Pollution**: how is this water loss? Well, it is the loss of water in which fish and plants can live—or can thrive.

Mills

Mills need a head of water. The water, flowing downhill, turns a wheel. Up in the hills, water is flowing down fast anyway, and no extra aid is needed. Lower down, the river may not be able to turn the wheel, and so a blockage is put in above the mill, so water can accumulate at a higher (upstream) level. This may just be in the watercourse, or may be in a man-made pond—anything to raise water level so that there is a head to turn the wheel. The wheel powers any simple process, from grinding corn to making weapons or paper.

This blockage may be called a "weir", a "dam" (usually earthen faced with stone), a "clyst(e)" or a "sluice" (with gates). These are now widespread English names, but earlier local names like "clyse" may persist in Somerset. The quantity of water passing through needs to be sufficient to turn the wheel, so an opening gate is advisable. In the (early) simple weirs, with a gap in the main weir, there was a moveable gate which was inserted into the gap, and locked the water upstream. This was the early lock. When in place, the head of water accumulated to turn the wheel. When the lock was removed, the water rushed through, the wheel turned—and, importantly, boats could pass through.

Quarrels inevitably ensued. The locked weirs stopped navigation. The open weir often did not create a sufficient head of water (whether natural, from slope, or artificial). Consequently the moveable lock on the weir developed. Obviously this was highly inefficient for both purposes, and subsequently the pound lock or bypass channel for boats, mill leat (pond and stream), and fish weirs and traps developed. The pound lock, or impounded lock system, is the one used today. This is two locking gates, the boat going into the one on its own level, having its gate closed, the other opened, and so with water pouring in or out, raising or lowering the boat. There are variants such as the East

Anglian staunch which—when working—had a divided channel, one side with a lock, the other with a weir.

Fish were once of such paramount importance, and river management between weirs and mills generally so low, that in the Industrial Revolution fish movement was not appreciably restricted. Now, however, without fish passes—and efficient ones!—fish, and much other aquatic life, have seriously declined or even becoming extinct.

"Mills, weirs and locks men do them call
That do annoy that worthy stream,
Against the law they all do stand
But still they drown those simple men."

(1585 Appeal to Queen Elizabeth I, in Thacker, 1914)

Fishing tended to be local to one landowner's part of the river. Navigation tended to be regional or national—but with poor enforcement, "might" often prevailed.

Magna Carta, 1215, as some may know, lays down the principles of justice in courts. What fewer know is that it devotes more words to navigation and fish weirs, mills, etc., than to abstract justice. (Interestingly, it also provides for protection of foreign merchants travelling by river if war should break out.)

Mills—do they count as produce from the river? Well, perhaps! They certainly produce goods and generate income. They are scattered over and around the Brue valley where those in the main Brue could have flow aided by locks to create power. Some remains of mills, or restored mills still exist, others are remembered by their names on maps and old documents.

The first water mills were flour mills, grinding corn (usually wheat—bread needs flour not wheat grains). That means grinding, which means energy. To do this by woman-power with a quern may take all day for a household. The women also cooked, cleaned, raised children, made clothes, and if available, looked after dairy (from milking to cheese-making), gardening, etc.. Removing the work of grinding—if it could be avoided by using water mills— allowed more time for more rewarding activities. Water mills came to England with the Romans, and by *Domesday Book* (1086) many of the major (late) ones were established. Windmills came later (and spread in the twelfth century).

Power now being available, mills were used for many other purposes. The mid-fourteenth century Black Death, which roughly halved the population, was a great incentive towards mechanisation for tanning, linen, crushing, sawing, coins, jewellery, weapons, forging metals, paper, paints, laundering, malt, fulling, cloth, dyeing, copper, brass, spinning, silk, iron, lead, snuff, silver, gold…anything, in fact, that was available. Rivers like the Brue would have had primarily corn mills, secondarily wool-related mills, plus others. Manufacture which did not use power was still likely to use water for transport, for supply, or for washing (whether as process or as cleaning) so many industrial and commercial enterprises favoured siting by and on rivers.

Fisheries, mills and navigation progressed, with much acrimony—quarrelling over boats, road travel, fishing and milling.

Pollution

Pollution, in the English definition, is changes caused by man-made alteration to the river chemistry (water or soil) which cause biological change. The Brue itself is now far from clean (see **River Vegetation** below).

Fisheries, corn mills and boats led only to mild pollution (general dirt, waste product disposal and such-like). However, tanning, fulling, laundering (most) and metalwork caused serious pollution. In the Quantock Hills, Somerset (but not the River Brue catchment) frequent fulling mills created gross pollution.

Pollution in the Brue Valley comes from agrochemical run-off, road run-off, and from waste, mostly rural and urban, and, formerly, the Puriton armaments; domestic waste (sewage and other from toothpaste to detergents) mostly from sewage treatment works, commercial and industrial (the last two minor, in this catchment). Even domestic waste is low, as there are no large towns. Even Wells, by comparison, is a small city.

Pollution may be of many kinds and many strengths. Plants and animals react differently to the type and strength of pollutants. For instance, green plant cells make oxygen, so oxygen deficiency which is high enough to kill a lot of invertebrates can leave the plants unaffected. Conversely, invertebrates are generally more sensitive to heavy metal pollution.

Vegetation pollution in the River Brue is considerable.

River Vegetation

Chalkstreams are a unique, valuable and very rare global habitat, and most are found in south and central England.

Chalk is a soft limestone, dating from the Cretaceous period, composed of tiny lime sea shells (*Foraminifera*) dropping to the sea floor when the inhabitants die. They live in unusually pure water, influenced by the calcium-rich shells, with little silt or other nutrient-rich influences from the land. As such it is unique, but even in England there are the soft limestone oolite streams of the (earlier) Jurassic period, which stretch across the east of England. These are smaller because on chalkstreams they tend to run along it, surrounded by chalk, whilst more often oolite ones cross the limestone, and flow on to clay (or other rock type, see Haslam, *The River Scene* (1997) or *Vegetation of British Rivers* (1982)), so having fairly small catchments. Then again chalk does not form mountains (too soft) whilst the main hard limestone (Carboniferous limestone) is like the oolite, not quite as pure limestone.

So what about the River Brue? The Combe Brook tributary is limestone with the characteristically-shaped Downs upstream, and a depauperate shadow of chalk vegetation—very common on oolite. The Brook does not now have enough water. This happens too often on limestone (and sandstone). The rock is porous, and underground water is stored and moved in aquifers. And along come developers demanding water for new housing. And indeed householders from old housing are using far more water than they did a century ago. So in go the pipes and pumps, and away goes the water which should be in the river. (There are ways of increasing river water even so, such as re-instating or instating frequent small weirs.) Runoff from rainfall is today limited in replenishing ground water as there is increased hard standing and roads and less gardens in new developments.

So here is one of those wonderful valuable streams: and is there any group conserving or restoring it to its original or at least traditional status? What a silly question! This is not a bittern, or a half canoe: why should anyone do anything? Let it disappear.

In fact the best limestone vegetation here is just outside the Brue catchment proper in the Cheddar Gorge stream, a tributary of the River Axe, which is on hard limestone. Whether it still carries enough water to turn a dozen mills in a quarter of a mile is uncertain, but there is certainly enough, despite all the disturbance, to give pockets of *Ranunculus*-based plant communities.

The River Sheppey rises on chalk but then flows on to clay. The Wells City tributary (River Chilcote) is also on hard limestone (reaching from the Mendips), but it is too low in other nutrients to resemble a soft-rock stream.

Outside Britain the largest European chalk outcrop is in north west France, but as this is covered over by a layer of desert sand (loess), it gives a sand and more nutrient-rich influence to its streams. There are pockets of lowland limestone with small lime streams. The (West and Central Europe) limestone streams that most resemble chalkstreams—given the geographic variation in vegetation anyway—are those of the lowland hard limestone of south east France, and the hard limestone ones to the east of the German Black Forest.

The River Brue catchment has a splendid diversity of watercourse vegetation (see Figs 45a, b), even excluding ponds, bogs, reedbeds and other wetland. There are of course small streams rising, especially upstream. The Brue itself, is of reasonable size, and in the wetland there are many dykes (rhynes) of various qualities. Apart from the upstream limestone, the Brue has tributary streams on clay and other assorted rock types as well as those on peat and alluvium in the wetland.

Near their sources the watercourses are not only narrow and small, but dry, with land plants. The upper Brue has little river vegetation. Where the streams appear to be dug out, they have been! Hedging and ditching was a common winter job on farms. With all the drying up, ditching is now infrequent. Further downstream, water becomes less seasonal: though run-off and flushes occur after rain. There may be springs where flowing water is perennial, emergent aquatic plants can grow, and once water is deep enough, water-supported species can enter also, provided disturbance, shade and pollution permit.

Bruton has much disturbance and little vegetation, apart from some good fringes of emergents, mostly tall monocotyledons like *Glyceria maxima* (reed sweet grass) (Fig. 42). Downstream of Bruton, however, the river, still only 4–8m wide, is suitable for a good diversity of clay-like vegetation, plus a little lime water. The vegetation from here to its passage into the Moors and Levels near Street is generally moderately good, with a diversity of up to 10 species in the main 1970s surveys. The *Ranunculus* shows the "light" clay (Lias) and lime influence, *Butomus umbellatus* (flowering rush), *Scirpus lacustris* (bulrush), *Nuphar lutea* (yellow water lily) and algal *Enteromorpha* show the more nutrient-rich influence. Altogether this was a satisfactory river.

Fig. 42. Near Gold Corner. Medium-sized wetland rhyne (vegetation adequate)

But by 2013 there had been a deplorable, almost catastrophic loss! The widespread collapse of *c.* 2000 has indeed happened here, and there is as yet (2019/20) little sign of recovery.

In this stretch of the Brue several sizeable tributaries have entered. The Combe brook (north) is lime (see above). Upstream the channel is dry, lower, there are patches of good vegetation. (The cone-shaped hill is interesting, like a small Glastonbury Tor.) The next tributary is the River Pitt (south), on light clay. The earlier good vegetation had gone by 2013. River Alham (to the north) is no better. Near its source round Upton Noble and Batcombe, lime influence brings *Rorippa nasturtium-aquaticum* (water cress) and *Apium nodiflorum* (fool's water cress) in water too shallow for water-supported species.

In its final stretch to the sea, the River Brue was in good condition in the 1970s, and was in fair condition in the 2010s (Figs 43, 44). Diversity is down. *Potamogetons* (pondweeds) and *Sagittaria sagittifolia* (Arrowhead), instead of being present at nearly all sites, and abundant at several, have almost gone. A reaction, according to Danish and German research, to using machines to cut and dredge. The 2013 records show little *Butomus umbellatus* too, but that and *Sagittaria* did appear later that summer, and at the normal time the year after, as seen, for example, in Figure 45a, b.

40

Fig. 43. Lower River Brue. A fringe of vegetation only

Fig. 44. Levels, farm bridge and road bridge

The wetland dyke—ditch, rhyne—irrigation/drainage system is more than a full study by itself, but briefly speaking these channels (Fig 45a, b) can be divided into (pages 44–45):

Distribution of Aquatic Plants R. Brue, Somerset 1974 & 1975

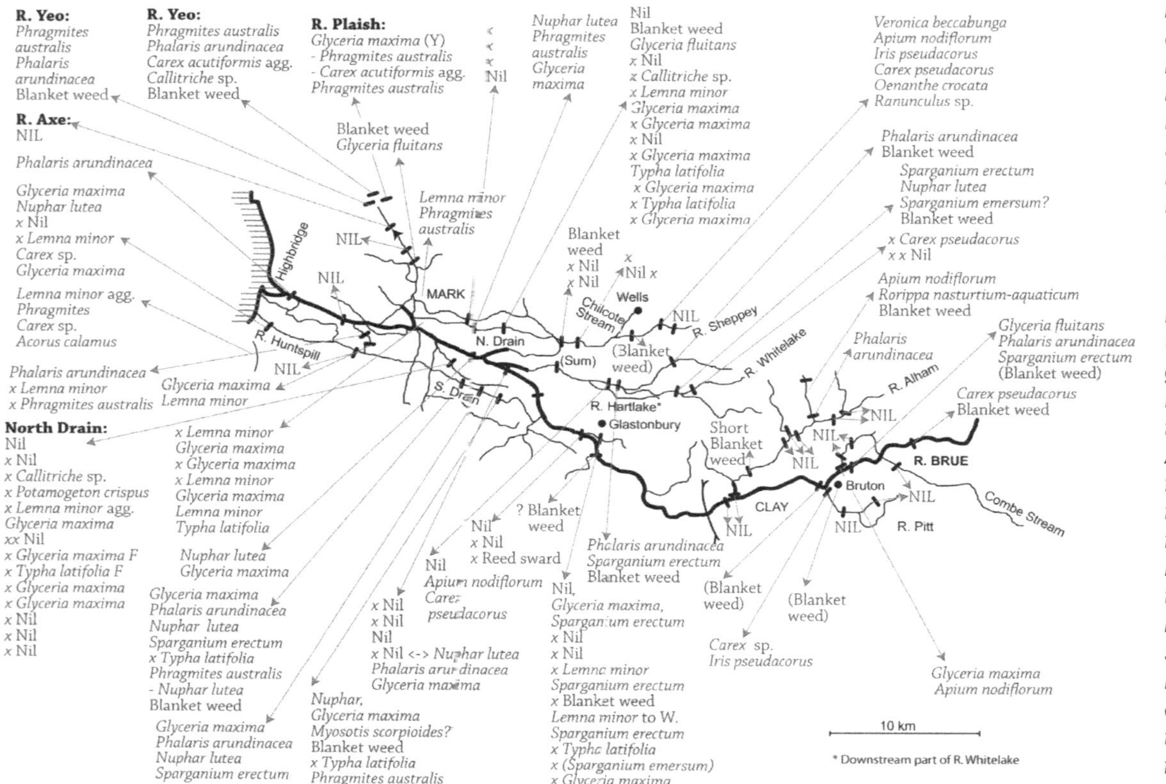

Distribution of Aquatic Plants R. Brue, Somerset 2013

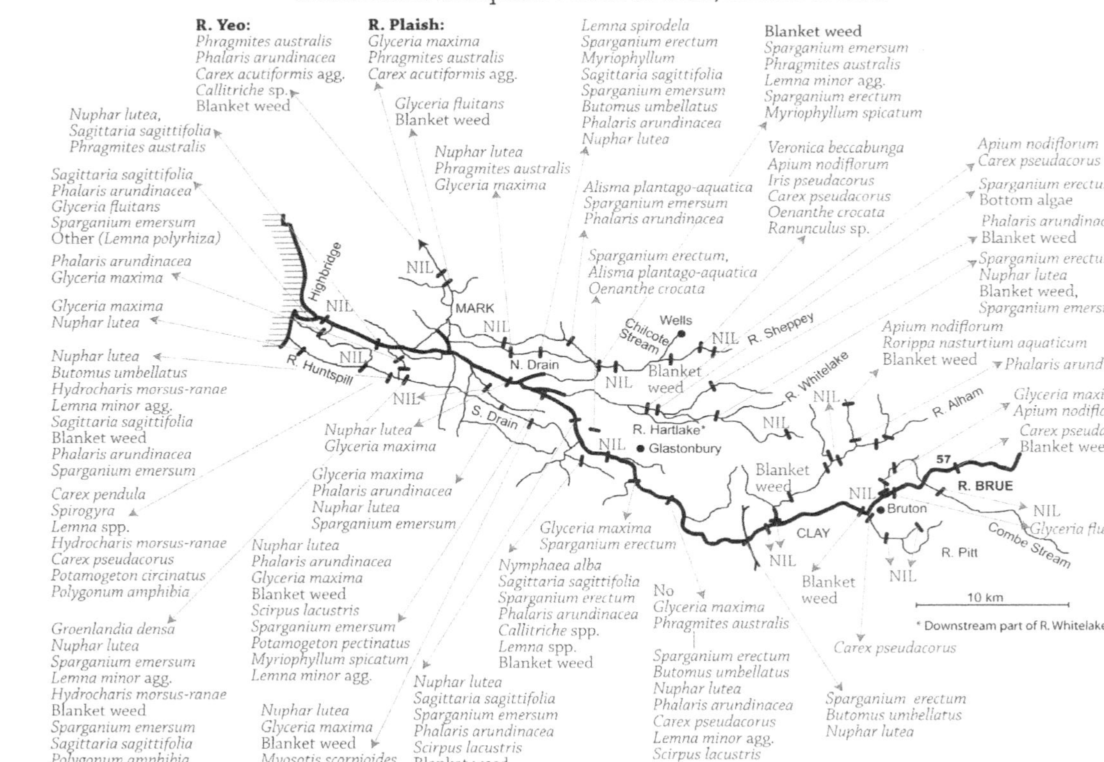

43

(1) **Dry**. These bear land plants and may even be filled in and visible only from a distance or from aerial photography. These show the historical drying of the area (no river plants remain).

(2) **Damp**. In summer, some with deep water, winter water often penned up from damp to deep with emergent vegetation, usually tall monocotyledons (has only one seed leaf) sometimes with a few shorter plants after cutting or dredging. Tall monocotyledons usually cast heavy shade, and are vigorous and competitive. *Glyceria maxima* is the most common dominant of the channel, or of edges of larger channels. It is also indicative of slightly less disturbance and intensive farming than *Phragmites australis* (common reed). This reflects the present influence from the moors. Most of the land is grassland, some is crops.

(3) **Having enough water to support floating and submerged plants, most or all of the year.** This depends as much on the controls as it does on the rain. *Lemna minor* agg. (Common duckweed) often covers and smothers the water (Fig. 46). This is typical of over-managed channels up to about 4m wide. Dense duckweed should be removed from channels with moving water, as it can block sluices, etc. Under smothering duckweed, diversity is usually very low. At the edges, other vegetation may be good and diverse, if slopes are gentle or moderate, or may have few or no aquatics if they are very steep or much disturbed, or if the water is polluted. Grazing of suitably-sloped channels may encourage diverse short emergents, or be too much and prevent them, or too little and allow tall monocotyledons to shade and kill them.

Fig. 46. Medium-small wetland rhyne. Vegetation sub-adequate (Lemna minor agg. dominant)

(4) **Channels in good condition**. The surface species are likely to include *Lemna trisulca* (the translucent duckweed that sits just below the water surface) and *Hydrocharis morsus-ranae* (Frogbit—the plant like an over-small water lily, but without a water lily flower), and probably 9–15 different species in all, in each 12m of dyke, at least 5 being water-supported species (Fig. 47). These channels are fewer than they used to be. Good vegetation still exists, but less of it. So who notices? Increased management may often kill river vegetation.

Fig. 47. Small wetland rhyne. Parts good vegetation (should be cleared in part)

Unluckily, although a few of the river plants have quite simple names like yellow water lily, far too many have English names that are not easy—fennel-leaved pondweed, for example. That in itself is possible, but when there are a dozen and more other pond weeds...?

The River Sheppey, like the River Alham, rises in hard limestone and has patches of limestone vegetation. The limestone influence of the tributary Chilcote stream is lost in the Moors and Levels, when flow becomes very slow and water is affected by the Moors and Levels. The rivers and the North and South Drains are used as drains so are much-managed and vegetation is poor. The Huntspill River was dug in 1940 to supply vast quantities of water for the munitions factory at Puriton. Creating the Huntspill river, by machine, caused destruction to the ecology. However, now that more is known about the damaging consequences of these former actions, and how these have affected the wildlife and aquatic plants, the authorities have inserted wildlife refuges

45

at intervals along the river. Fortunately, as the river was constructed with wide flood banks, the horseshoe-shaped breaks in which tall emergents, short emergents and even water-supported plants could grow, could be made without damaging its structure. Once a stable habitat is established, plants can creep slowly out: until swept away by water, weed-cutting boats or whatever. The original refuge inhabitants may well remain and the cycle starts again.

Daniel Defoe (novelist, traveller and government agent) toured "The Whole Island of Great Britain" (Defoe 1724–26; 1962). This was in the early eighteenth century on the cusp of the Industrial Revolution when water (and wind) power were at their height, and steam power—which is less tied with water, though water was advisable for washing, cooling , etc.—was about to spread. Roughly, the lower Levels area (including part of the lower Brue valley) bore black cattle, the lush pastures of the rest of the county, sheep. The number of looms, though, was greater even than the great amount of wool produced in the county, and more was imported from all over the region. Vast quantities of different kinds of textiles were exported to Europe as well as the rest of Britain. Wells, Shepton Mallett and Glastonbury, all Brue Towns, were particularly known for knitted stockings (principally for export to Spain!). Brimpton, Shepton Mallett (and Castle Cary) made clothing and exported it through Europe from Sweden to Italy.

This explains the comfortable and varying housing along the high streets: comfortable houses for well-off artisans, and more-than comfortable manor houses outside the village. Incidentally, Defoe notes that, exceptionally, every child of five upwards "could earn its own living—by weaving".

Indeed a fascinating, and unique, riverscape!

REFERENCES

A short history of Brewham URL: http://www.brewham.co.uk/ brewhams-history, September 2017. (Accessed 8 September 2019)

Brunning, R. 2006. *Wet and Wonderful.* Somerset Heritage Service, Taunton.

Brunning, R. & Farr-Cox, F. 2005. The River Siger rediscovered. *Archaeology in the Severn Estuary*, 16, 7–15.

Defoe, D. (1724-26). *A Tour Through the Whole Island of Great Britain* (English Library, 1962).

Bunyan, J. 1694. *The Pilgrim's Progress.*

Haslam, S.M. 1982. *Vegetation of British Rivers.* Nature Conservancy Council, London.

Haslam, S.M. 1991. *The Historic River.* Cobden of Cambridge Press, Cambridge.

Haslam, S.M. 1997. *The River Scene.* University Press, Cambridge.

Haslam, S.M. 2010. *A Book of Reed.* Forrest Press, Cardigan.

Hill-Cottingham, P.; Briggs, D.; Brunning, R.; King, A.; & Rix, G. (eds). 2006. *Somerset Books*, Wellington.

Pannett, D.J. 1981. "Fish Weirs of the River Severn". In *Evolution of Marshland Landscapes.* University Department of External Studies, Oxford, pp. 144–152.

Pevsner, N. 1958, 2003 (ed.). *Buildings of England. South and West Somerset.* Penguin. Yale University Press, New Haven.

Rippon, S. 1997. *The Severn Estuary. Landscape evolution and wetland reclamation.* Leicester University Press.

Rippon, S. (ed.). 2001. *Estuarine Archaeology: the Severn and beyond.* The Severn Estuary.

Rippon, S. 2004. *Making the most of a bad situation.* 'Glastonbury Abbey, Meare on the Medieval Exploitation of wetland resources in the Somerset Levels'.

Rippon, S. & Cameron, N. 2006. *Landscape community and colonisation: the north Somerset Levels.* Council for British Archaeology.

Thacker, F. 1914. *Thames Highway*, Volume I, from "Where Thames Smooth Waters Glide" (1585 Appeal to Queen Elizabeth I).

Victoria County History, Vols. 8, 9. (Founded 1899.)

Williams, M. 1970. *The draining of the Somerset Levels.* University Press, Cambridge.

Wolseley, P.A., Palmer, M.A., & Williams, R. 1984. *The aquatic flora of the Somerset Levels and Moors.* Nature Conservancy Council, England.

THE RIVER FRIEND SERIES

This series of small books is designed for people with a general or specific interest in rivers.
Please visit the River Friend Website for an up to-date list of
PUBLISHED Titles: **http://www.riverfriend.tinasfineart.uk /home**

Standalone Titles in the Series include:

A PROLOGUE TO THE SERIES: Plant identification and Glossary of Terms
(ISBN 978 1 9162096 2 6)

DRYING UP (ISBN 978 1 9162096 1 9)

STREAM STORY I: A Riveting Riverscape—River Brue, Somerset
(ISBN 978 1 9162096 0 2)

INTERPRET: What do Plants Tell us? (ISBN 978 1 9162096 5 7)

Vegetation Changes Over Time. Is there FREEZE FRAME?
(ISBN 978 1 9162096 6 4)

REED—ON THE EDGE (ISBN 978 1 9162096 4 0)

An Introduction to the WATER FRAMEWORK DIRECTIVE
(ISBN 978 1 9162096 3 3)

WATER: Clean and Dirty (ISBN 978 1 9162096 7 1)

STREAM STORY II: A Brook in Transit: Bourn Brook, Cambs
(ISBN 978 1 9162096 8 8)

CHANGE: What a Disaster! (ISBN 978 1 9162096 9 5)

LOOK AT THE BOTTOM

How to lose Fresh Water in Under Two Centuries. The Example of MALTA

VEGETATION PATTERNS

IN THE WATER

THE WATERS OF WELLS

RESTORE, REHABILITATE, IMPROVE

AWFUL ALIENS

About the Authors

Sylvia Haslam is a botanist and river culture, etc., specialist. Anyone wanting to find out more should look at the publications list on her website (http://www.riversandreeds.co.uk). Her publications specific to this series are listed in the book entitled *A PROLOGUE TO THE SERIES: Plant identification and Glossary of Terms*.

Tina Bone has worked as a self-employed Desktop Publisher for many years until she changed career to work as a Professional Artist from March 2005. To view Tina's resumé and artwork please visit her website: http://www.tinasfineart.uk.